Whose FEET Are These?

Written and Photographed by
Wayne Lynch

Gareth Stevens Publishing
A WORLD ALMANAC EDUCATION GROUP COMPANY

Please visit our web site at: www.garethstevens.com
For a free color catalog describing Gareth Stevens Publishing's
list of high-quality books and multimedia programs, call
1-800-542-2595 (USA) or 1-800-387-3178 (Canada).
Gareth Stevens Publishing's fax: (414) 332-3567.

Library of Congress Cataloging-in-Publication Data

Lynch, Wayne.
    Whose feet are these? / written and photographed by Wayne Lynch.
       p. cm. — (Name that animal!)
    Includes bibliographical references and index.
    Summary: Photographs and descriptions of their feet serve as clues to help
the reader identify different animals; also includes information on the physical
characteristics and behavior of each animal.
    ISBN 0-8368-3640-5 (lib. bdg.)
    1. Foot—Juvenile literature.   2. Animals—Juvenile literature.
(1. Animals. 2. Foot.) I. Title.
QL950.7.L96   2003
591.47'9—dc21   2002036533

This edition first published in 2003 by
Gareth Stevens Publishing
A World Almanac Education Group Company
330 West Olive Street, Suite 100
Milwaukee, Wisconsin 53212 USA

This U.S. edition © 2003 by Gareth Stevens, Inc. Original edition © 1999 by
Wayne Lynch. First published in 1999 by Whitecap Books, Vancouver.
Additional end matter © 2003 by Gareth Stevens, Inc.

Gareth Stevens series editor: Dorothy L. Gibbs
Gareth Stevens graphic designer: Katherine A. Goedheer

Printed in the United States of America

1 2 3 4 5 6 7 8 9 07 06 05 04 03

T hink about all the things you can do with your feet. You can run, jump, dance, pedal a bicycle, even balance on a skateboard and do awesome tricks.

Although the feet of wild animals look very different from yours, they can use them to run and jump just like you. Wild animals can also use their feet to dig, climb, hunt, or protect themselves.

Can you name the wild animals whose feet are pictured in this book?

The skin on the bottom of my feet is bumpy. It looks a lot like sandpaper. Because I like to eat buds, new leaves, twigs, and bark, I spend a lot of time in trees. When I climb trees, the bark is often wet and slippery. My rough feet help me hold onto the branches so I do not fall and hurt myself.

Who am I?

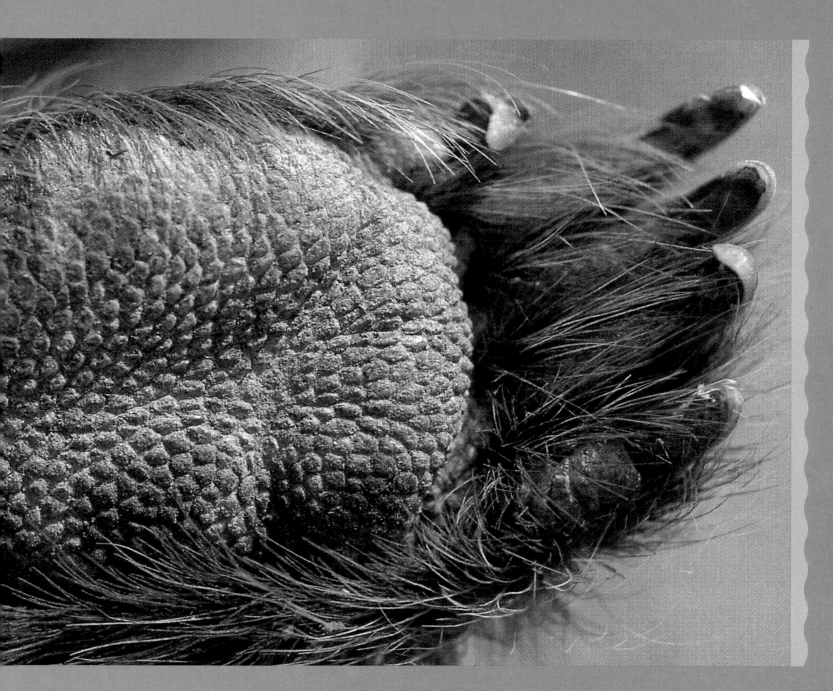

I am a porcupine. I live in the forests of North America. I am round and fat, so I cannot run very fast. My body is covered with long, sharp needles, called quills, to protect me from wolves, bears, and coyotes. When I am attacked, I swat the enemy with my spiny tail.

Porcupines love salt! They often make campers angry by eating the salty wood on boat oars and shovel handles.

I am one of the biggest birds in the world. I weigh as much as a small woman. I cannot fly, but my strong legs and feet make me a speedy runner. Each of my feet has three toes. My inside toes have long claws at the tips. When I have to fight, my claws are good weapons.

Who am I?

I am a cassowary. I live in the rain forests of New Guinea, which is near Australia. Even though I can defend myself with my feet, I usually hide when I hear anything coming. I eat mushrooms, ripe fruit, and creepy crawlies, such as snails, worms, and centipedes.

A cassowary has a thick helmet on the top of its head. This hard helmet protects the bird as it races through the forest.

My bright orange feet help me swim through the ocean, and when I dive for food, I use my feet to steer. I am an expert diver and can hold my breath for up to six minutes. I cannot fly like most birds, but I use my small, stiff wings like flippers to "fly" underwater.

Who am I?

I am a penguin. I live in Antarctica, which is the ice-covered continent at the South Pole. Although I have a thick coat of feathers, I still get cold in the icy ocean. To keep warm, I eat lots of squid, fish, and shrimp — my favorite foods.

In a single dive, a penguin can swallow as many as one hundred shrimp. Its tongue and the top of its mouth have stiff spines that help the penguin hold on to slippery foods.

Where I live, it can snow any day of the year. My hooves have sharp edges to dig through crusty snow so I can reach the plants I like to eat. Because I have very long hair, the Inuit people call me *oomingmak,* which means "bearded one." I also have strong horns that help me fight off hungry wolves and polar bears.

Who am I?

I am a male musk ox. I live in the cold Arctic. My long hair covers my whole body and hangs around my legs like a warm, shaggy skirt. In summer, I shed my thick coat. Big clumps of wool fall off and blow away. Small birds often collect the wool for their nests.

In fall, male musk oxen fight for females by ramming each other with their curved, sharply pointed horns.

L ike the rest of my body, my feet are covered with tough, scaly skin. My feet are small, so they are useful only for crawling onto land, where I warm my body in the Sun and digest my meals. I like to eat birds, large snakes, and fish, especially piranhas. Even these fierce fish cannot hurt my tough skin.

Who am I?

I am a caiman. I live in the lakes and rivers of South America. Like my close relative the alligator, I swim by sweeping my long, powerful tail from side to side. I have many sharp teeth, but I cannot chew my food with them. I often swallow my meals in one large gulp.

When food is hard to find, a caiman can live for many months on the fat stored in its long tail.

The claws on my front feet can grow to be as long as a ballpoint pen. They are longer than the claws of any other animal. I use my long claws like a rake to dig up roots or to dig out ground squirrels. These are two of my favorite foods. I also use my claws like a shovel to dig my winter den.

Who am I?

I am a grizzly bear. I live in the forests of North America and Asia. In fall, I stuff myself with berries and salmon, too, if I am near their rivers. In winter, I hibernate, which is like sleeping. I do not eat or drink while I am hibernating, so when I wake up in spring, I am very hungry!

If a big male grizzly stood on its hind legs inside your house, its head would touch the ceiling.

Each winter, I grow thick, warm feathers on my feet and toes, and my toenails grow longer. The feathers work like snowshoes and keep me from sinking into the snow when I walk. I need long toenails to scrape through crusty snow so I can reach the small seeds and plants I like to eat.

Who am I?

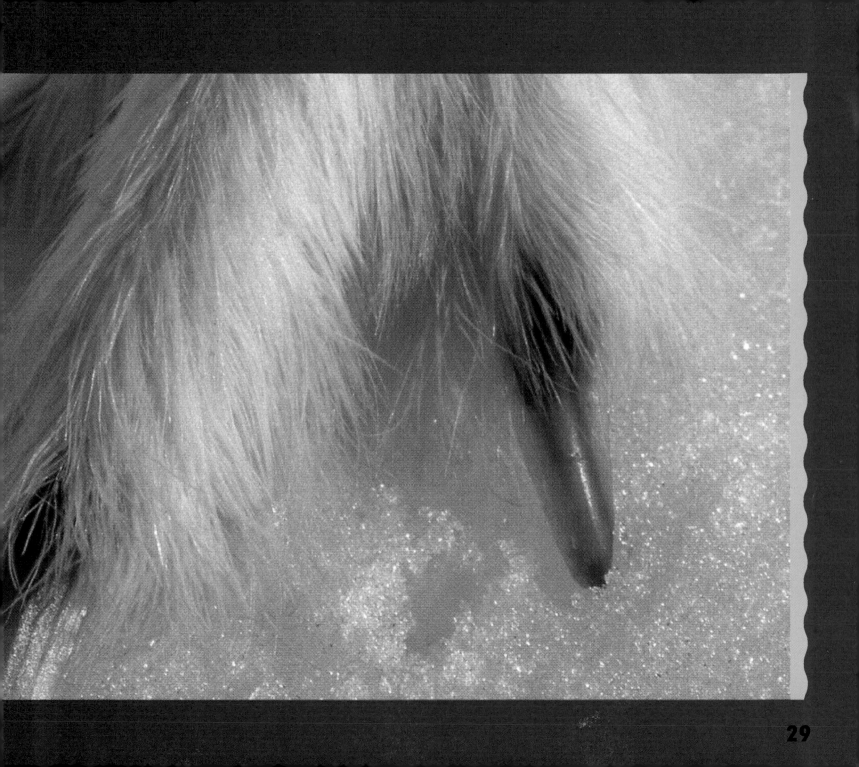

I am a ptarmigan (pronounced *TAR-muh-gan*). I live in the Arctic. I look like a wild chicken, but in winter, most of my feathers turn white. My white feathers hide me in the snow, protecting me from hungry foxes, wolves, and snowy owls. I live in a large flock, and we all watch for danger.

On winter nights, a ptarmigan will often bury itself in the snow so it can sleep out of the wind.

Index

More Books to Read

Animal Feet. Look Once, Look Again (series). David M. Schwartz (Gareth Stevens)

Feet That Suck and Feed. Diane Swanson (Greystone Books)

Paws and Claws. Elizabeth Miles (Heinemann Library)

Whose Feet Are These: A Look at Hooves, Paws, and Claws. Peg Hall (Picture Window Books)